My Little PATIENT PEBBLE

PETER PAUPER PRESS, INC.
Rye Brook, New York

PETER PAUPER PRESS

In 1928, at the age of twenty-two, Peter Beilenson began printing books on a small press in the basement of his parents' home in Larchmont, New York. Peter—and later, his wife, Edna—sought to create fine books that sold at "prices even a pauper could afford."

Today, still family owned and operated, Peter Pauper Press continues to honor our founders' legacy of quality, value, and fun for big kids and small kids alike.

Written by Hannah Beilenson
Designed by Heather Zschock

3 International Drive
Rye Brook, NY 10573 USA

Published in the UK and Europe by Peter Pauper Press, Inc.
c/o White Pebble International
Units 2-3, Spring Business Park
Stanbridge Road
Havant, Hampshire PO9 2GJ, UK

ISBN 978-1-4413-4209-6
Printed in China

7 6 5 4 3 2 1

Visit us at www.peterpauper.com

OUR ACTIONS AND US

Have you ever tried something new? Shared a toy or snack? Given a hug or high five when someone needed it? Well, those are just a few examples of putting your feelings into action! And every action you take can make a change. You can make people smile and laugh, help others feel safe, and create something new for everyone to share. There's so much you can do, and there's no wrong place to start—so let's take action today!

One action is **Patience**, and we'll meet someone who will help us learn more about it.

I wish my mom would hurry up.
I can't wait to go to the lake!
Me neither.

Who are you?
I'm a **Patient Pebble**.
What's "patience"?

Patience is when you're able
to wait for something,
even when it's hard.

I'm meeting some friends at the lake,
but it's taking me a long time to get there.

It's taking me a long time
to get there, too! My mom
says we can't go until she
finishes some chores.

I HATE WAITING!

Showing patience can be hard. But did you know that waiting can lead to good things, too?
Really?

Yes! Would you rather wait for a cake to bake all the way through, or eat it when it's not done?
Hmm. Well, I guess it tastes better when it's fully baked.

And when you finish a painting, do you want to hang it up right away, or wait for it to dry?
I don't want to smudge my art, so I wait for it to dry.

I think I get it—sometimes I need to wait to have the most fun.
Exactly!

But waiting doesn't always lead to more fun,
and it's so hard!

I hate waiting in line.

And I hate long car rides.

I know what you mean. But sometimes you have to stand in line, or go to places that are far away. Practicing patience can make waiting a little easier.

How do I practice patience?
You can distract yourself to pass the time!

You can listen
to music,

draw, color, and write,

or even just observe the world around you.

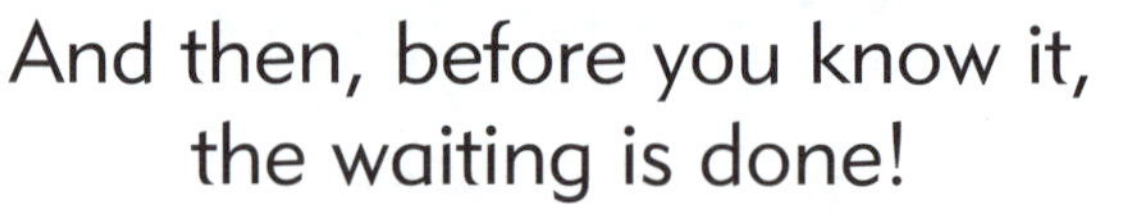
And then, before you know it, the waiting is done!
Wow, we're here! And there are your friends.

Thank you
for helping me
be patient.
No problem! And thank you
for taking me to my friends.

Meet My Patient Pebble

My Patient Pebble's name is:

....

I need to wait when:

....

....

....

I can practice patience by:

....

....

....

....